CREATURES
WE CAN'T LIVE
WITHOUT

We Need
BACTERIA

KATIE KAWA

PowerKiDS
press

New York

Published in 2016 by The Rosen Publishing Group, Inc.
29 East 21st Street, New York, NY 10010

First Edition

Editor: Caitie McAneney
Book Design: Mickey Harmon

Photo Credits: Cover (image) Tishchenko Irina/Shutterstock.com; cover, pp. 1, 3, 4, 8–10, 13, 16, 19, 22–24 (background) Click Bestsellers/Shutterstock.com; p. 5 (main) Darren Baker/Shutterstock.com; p. 5 (inset) StudioSmart/ Shutterstock.com; pp. 6–7 (main) Volodymyr Goinyk/Shutterstock.com; p. 6 (desert) ventrdusud /Shutterstock.com; p. 6 (city) Songquan Deng/Shutterstock.com; p. 8 (inset) www.royaltystockphoto.com/Shutterstock.com; p. 9 (spiral) Stocktrek Images/Stocktrek Images/Getty Images; p. 9 (rods) martynowi.cz /Shutterstock.com; p. 9 (spheres) Knorre/iStock/Getty Images; p. 11 (main) Lukiyanova Natalia/frenta/Shutterstock.com; p. 11 (inset) Sergey Panteleev/E+/Getty Images; p. 12 Richard Griffin/ Shutterstock.com; p. 14 (inset) MichaelTayor3d/Shutterstock.com; pp. 14–15 Sebastian Kaulitzki/Shutterstock.com; p. 17 Blend Images/ERproductions Ltd/Vetta/Getty Images; p. 18 wavebreakmedia/Shutterstock.com; p. 20 (inset) irur/Shutterstock.com; pp. 20–21 Bullstar/Shutterstock.com.

Library of Congress Cataloging-in-Publication Data

Kawa, Katie, author.
  We need bacteria / Katie Kawa.
     pages cm. — (Creatures we can't live without)
Includes bibliographical references and index.
ISBN 978-1-4994-0978-9 (pbk.)
ISBN 978-1-4994-1001-3 (6 pack)
ISBN 978-1-4994-1020-4 (library binding)
1. Bacteria—Juvenile literature. 2. Host-bacteria relationships—Juvenile literature. I. Title.
QR57.K39 2016
579.3—dc23
                                        2014050041

Manufactured in the United States of America

CPSIA Compliance Information: Batch #WS15PK: For Further Information contact Rosen Publishing, New York, New York at 1-800-237-9932

CONTENTS

BACTERIA ARE EVERYWHERE!

Sometimes we try to get rid of the creatures we need the most. These creatures might scare you, or maybe you just think they're gross. Bacteria are creatures that many people think do nothing but spread sickness. However, many kinds of bacteria are actually helpful.

Bacteria are tiny **organisms** with only one **cell**. They come in different shapes. They're so small they can't be seen by human eyes. They can only be seen with a **microscope**. Bacteria are all around us. They live everywhere—from water and soil to the inside of our bodies. In fact, there are more bacteria in a person's body than cells!

CREATURE CLUE

There are about 100 trillion bacteria living in your **intestines**!

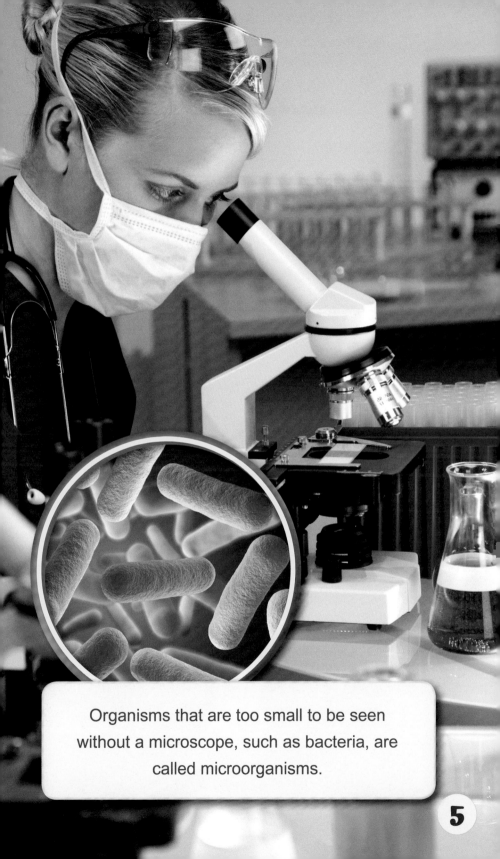

Organisms that are too small to be seen without a microscope, such as bacteria, are called microorganisms.

Bacteria can be found in all these very different habitats.

VERY OLD ORGANISMS

Microorganisms such as bacteria are the oldest forms of life on Earth. Scientists believe bacteria first appeared on Earth nearly 3.5 billion years ago. They can tell this by looking at **fossils** of bacteria, some of which are considered among the world's oldest fossils.

Because bacteria have been living on Earth for so long, they've **adapted** to life in almost every kind of habitat, or place where organisms can live. Some species, or kinds, of bacteria live in ice. Others live in water that's close to boiling. There are millions of bacteria in one spoonful of healthy soil!

CREATURE CLUE

Some species of bacteria live in clouds!

PARTS OF A BACTERIUM

Plants and animals are made up of many cells, but bacteria have only one cell. Each of these is called a bacterium. These cells look much different than those you would find in a plant or animal.

CREATURE CLUE

Some bacteria move with the help of body parts that look like tails. They're called flagella. A single tail is called a flagellum.

FLAGELLUM

Plant and animal cells have a part called the nucleus, which is like the brain of the cell. It holds the cell's DNA, which controls what the cell does. A bacterium doesn't have a nucleus in its cell. Instead, DNA is spread throughout the cell. The DNA still controls the cell, though. Bacteria also have a cell wall. This gives each bacterium its shape.

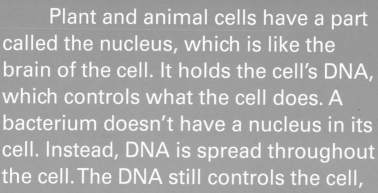

SPIRALS

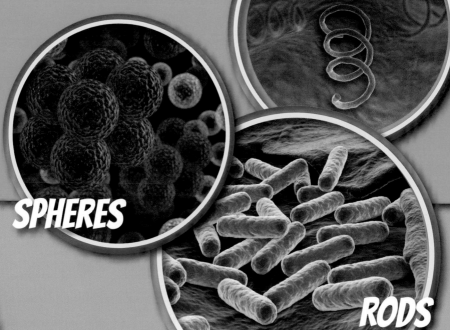

SPHERES

RODS

Bacteria are shaped like rods, spirals, or spheres (balls). The cell wall gives a bacterium one of these three shapes.

MAKING MORE BACTERIA

People often worry about the spread of harmful bacteria because it can happen so quickly. Bacteria reproduce, or make new bacteria, in different ways depending on their species. Some grow new bacteria inside a mother cell. Others reproduce by budding.

Most bacteria reproduce using a **process** called binary fission. For a cell to reproduce this way, it must first grow to twice its size. It must also make a copy of its DNA. Then, it breaks in two. This makes a new cell with the same DNA. A group of bacteria from the same mother cell are called a colony.

CREATURE CLUE

Budding happens when a growth, or bud, from one organism breaks away and becomes its own organism.

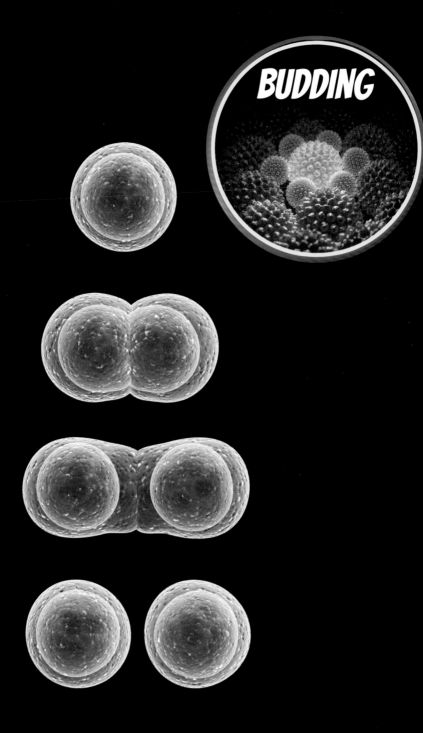

BUDDING

This bacterium is reproducing by splitting in two through the process of binary fission.

Plants give us food and oxygen, which is a gas humans need to live. We need bacteria in the soil because we need healthy plants.

WHAT'S A DECOMPOSER?

Bacteria play an important part in all ecosystems, or communities of living things. One place where they're especially helpful is in the soil. We need the trillions of bacteria that live in the soil. Without them, the soil wouldn't have the **nutrients** plants need to grow in it.

Bacteria in soil are decomposers. These are organisms that break down the bodies of dead plants and animals. As they break the bodies down, they put nutrients back into the soil. Plants take in these nutrients through their roots and use them to grow.

CREATURE CLUE

The smell of fresh soil comes from the bacteria that live in it.

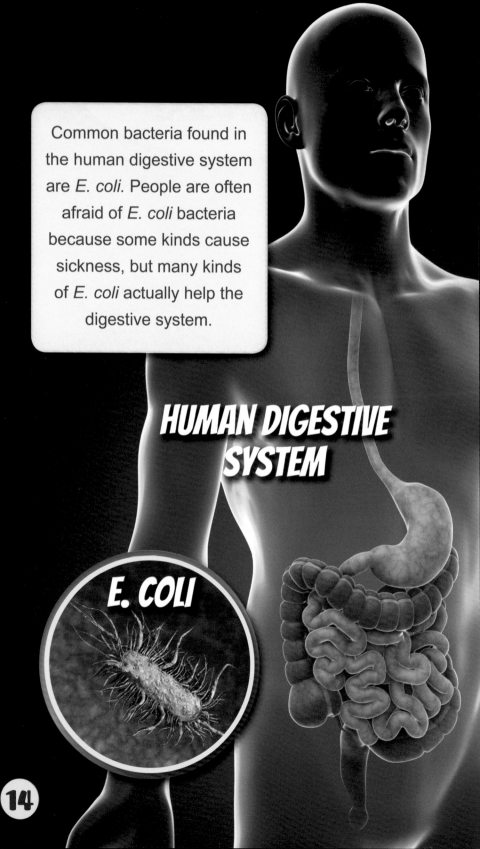

Common bacteria found in the human digestive system are *E. coli*. People are often afraid of *E. coli* bacteria because some kinds cause sickness, but many kinds of *E. coli* actually help the digestive system.

HUMAN DIGESTIVE SYSTEM

E. COLI

BREAKING DOWN YOUR FOOD

Bacteria are also an important part of the human digestive system. This is the group of **organs** that breaks down the food we eat. The digestive system is also called the gut, and bacteria living here are sometimes called gut bacteria. While harmful bacteria in your digestive system might give you a stomachache, most bacteria that live in this part of the body are there to help you.

Bacteria in the digestive system work to help the body break down food and get the nutrients it needs. These helpful bacteria also work to **protect** the digestive system from harmful bacteria that can cause sicknesses.

CREATURE CLUE

Helpful bacteria in the digestive system can come from the foods we eat, such as yogurt. Helpful bacteria are sometimes called probiotics.

KEEPING YOU HEALTHY

Bacteria also play an important part in the human body's immune system. The immune system is the part of the body that protects against organisms that don't belong in the body, including those that cause sickness. The immune system is made up of special cells whose only job is to protect the body.

Scientists have found that having certain bacteria in the body helps immune cells grow and multiply. Without bacteria, our immune system would be much weaker, and we would get sick more often. Bacteria actually help us stay healthy!

CREATURE CLUE

The digestive system is home to between 70 to 80 percent of the human body's immune cells.

Bacterial vaccines also help the immune system. A bacterial vaccine is a weakened form of a sickness-causing bacterium that's put into a person's body. Their body then learns to protect itself from that sickness.

If a person takes too many antibiotics, they can hurt their immune system and digestive system because these drugs kill too many good bacteria.

KILLING BACTERIA

While most bacteria are helpful, bad bacteria we call "germs" often make people very sick. People can get bacterial **infections**, which harm body parts such as skin.

People try to get rid of harmful bacteria in many different ways. Antibacterial products such as soaps are used to kill bacteria on our skin. Antibiotics are drugs taken to kill bacteria in our body when they make us sick. Both help people get rid of harmful bacteria. However, antibacterial products and antibiotics don't know which bacteria are helpful and which are harmful. They can kill good bacteria in our bodies, too.

CREATURE CLUE

Some harmful bacteria have become resistant to antibiotics. This means the drugs are no longer able to kill them.

Scientists are always trying to learn more about both harmful and helpful kinds of bacteria.

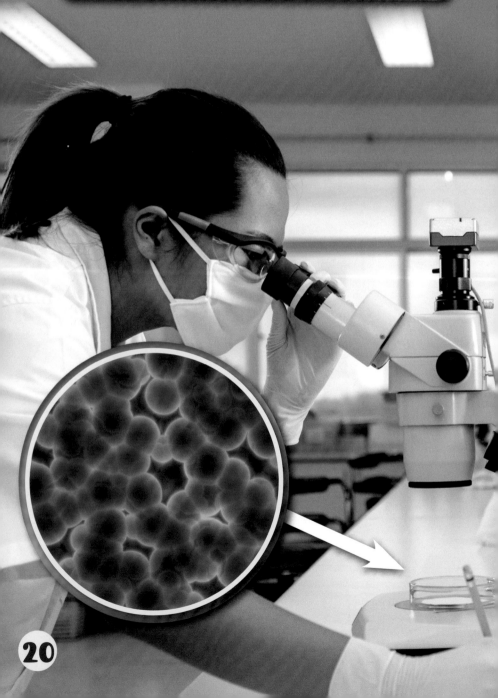

MORE HELPFUL THAN HARMFUL

Bacteria are found everywhere on Earth, and that's a good thing. They help plants grow in nutrient-rich soil, they help break down the food we eat, and they even help make that food. Certain kinds of bacteria are especially helpful in turning milk into cheese and yogurt.

Sometimes people need to kill bacteria that make them sick. In order to keep their body from losing too many good bacteria, they can eat foods that put good bacteria back into their body, such as yogurt. Good bacteria need to be protected because we can't live without them!

CREATURE CLUE

Different kinds of bacteria are used to make different kinds of cheese. They're also used to make pickles, olives, bread, and more!

How do bacteria help us?

SOIL

- break down dead plants and animals
- put nutrients back into the soil so plants can grow and give us food and oxygen

FOOD

- used to turn milk into cheese and yogurt
- used to make pickles, olives, and other foods

DIGESTIVE SYSTEM

- break down food into nutrients needed by the body
- protect digestive system from harmful bacteria and other organisms

IMMUNE SYSTEM

- cause immune cells to grow and reproduce
- help protect the body from sicknesses through bacterial vaccines

GLOSSARY

adapt: To change to fit new conditions.

cell: The smallest basic part of a living thing.

fossil: The hardened remains or trace of a living thing from a long time ago.

infection: A sickness caused by germs.

intestine: A long, winding tube in the human body that is made up of the small intestine and the large intestine. It helps the body take in nutrients from food and prepares waste to leave the body.

microscope: An instrument that uses lenses to show very small objects up close.

nutrient: Something taken in by a plant or animal that helps it grow and stay healthy.

organ: A body part that does a certain task.

organism: A living thing.

process: A series of actions or changes.

protect: To keep safe.

INDEX

WEBSITES